C IV

POEMS BY CID CORMAN

AND THE
WORD

COFFEE HOUSE PRESS :: Minneapolis :: 1987

The publishers thank the National Endowment for the
Arts, a federal agency, for a Small Press Assistance Grant,
and the Dayton Hudson Foundation for funds from
Dayton's and Target stores that aided in the production of
this book.

Coffee House Press books are available to bookstores and
libraries through our primary distributor: Consortium
Book Sales and Distribution, 213 East Fourth Street, Saint
Paul, Minnesota 55101. Our books are also available
through most other small-press distributors and through
all major library jobbers. For personal orders, catalogues,
and other information, write to Coffee House Press, Box
10870, Minneapolis, Minnesota 55458.

Library of Congress Cataloging in Publication Data

Corman, Cid.
  And the word.

  I. Title.
PS3553.065A66   1987   811'.54   87-18182
ISBN 0-918273-34-X (pbk. : alk. paper)

For Nancy Potter

How thank
without straining
pity

Letting
the petals fallen
taste earth

I

Anyone can play the poet –
get language to sit up and beg –
carry the news or lie down – all

feet at one's foot – making it seem
the easiest thing in the world –
as in a sense – if you can speak –

it is. But poetry occurs
in unanticipated ways –
bites and sniffs and keeps an eye on

spiritual territory.
Lets you know of what encroachments
bodies incur when they are free

of gross impediments. Enough
that when the poet himself has
done his thing and left his breath to

yours – you're not intended to sound
his praises – weep – or bestow on
him supervacuous honors.

4

The friends who know me
Bring their brew along
Under the pine trees
A few cups cure us
Deft old hands telling
Pouring it all out
Lost to self as such
No longer too much
Who knows where we are
Wine is far enough

All is a phantom: this we must bear –
Naked and barren as the air –
For us there are only others to care:
God's love we have wasted – ours we must share.

A god and yet a man,
A maiden yet a mother:
Wit wonders what wit can
Conceive this or the other.

A god and can he die?
A dead man, can he live?
What wit can well reply?
What reason reason give?

God, Truth itself, doth teach it.
Man's wit sinks too far under
By reason's power to reach it:
Believe and leave to wonder.

The power of Piero's
Resurrection biding in
its powerlessness rising

before our eyes even yet –
awakening the sense of
something beyond ourselves and

beyond those wooden soldiers
lying there by the box and
beyond the figure itself –

in those eyes beyond sleep and
beyond all declaration –
finding the frame no longer

holds as he enters into
us as we find ourselves the
opening through which he moves.

So others also
hear in Shinoda fields at
temple twilight snow

Sir – I have employed my time –
besides ditching – finishing
correcting amending and

transcribing my Travels in
four parts complete – augmented –
and intended for the press

when the world shall merit them –
or a printer shall be found
brave enough to risk his ears.

I like the idea of
meeting after distresses
and dispersions – but the end

I propose myself always
is to vex the world rather
than divert it – and if I

could compass that design and
not hurt my own person or
fortune I would be the most

indefatigable of
penmen you have ever seen
without reading. Now that your

genius is better engaged –
when you think of the world – please
give it one lash the more at

my request. I hate nations –
professions – communities –
and all my love is toward

individuals. Chiefly
I detest that animal
called man though I heartily

love John – Peter – Thomas and
so forth. I have almost done
with harridans and shall soon

be old enough to love girls
of fourteen. The lady whom
you describe to live at Court

to be deaf and no party
woman I take to be myth
but beyond moralizing.

She cannot be Mercy for
Mercy is neither deaf nor
lives at Court. Justice is blind

and perhaps deaf and neither
is she a Court lady. Now
Fortune *is* both blind and deaf

and a Court lady but then
she is a most damnable
bitch and will never make me

easy – as you promise. It
must be Riches – which answer
all your description. I am

glad she visits you but my
voice is so weak I doubt she
will ever hear me. I hear

of Dr. Arbuthnot's poor
health – a very sensible
affliction to me who have

lived so long out of the world
as to have lost that hardness
of heart contracted by years

and too much conversation.
I am daily losing friends
nor seek or get others. Oh!

if the world had a dozen
Arbuthnots in it I would
burn my Travels. However

he is not without fault. Our
Doctor has every gift
and virtue can make a man

amiable or useful
but alas! he has a sort of
slouch in his walk. I pray God

12

protect him for he is an
excellent Christian – though not
a Catholic – and as fit

a man either to live or
die as ever I knew. Are
you altogether these days

a country gentleman that
I must address you out of
London to the hazard of

losing this precious letter
which I will now conclude though
much paper is left. I have

an ill name and therefore shall
not subscribe it but you will
guess it comes from one who does

esteem and love you about
half as much as you deserve –
I mean as much as he can.

Here we are again –
moon – on the hill at
year's end. Seeing you –

knowing you still there –
as you are – helps. A
mite. Sick as I was

I'm sicker. But – moon –
I do remember
a time I didnt

know I knew – of hope –
and nothing to look
backward to or from.

But memory is
memory as this
this. And this heart hurts.

MIDWAY

Yellow pears and hosts
of wild roses
leaning out over the lake –
O beautiful swans –
giddy from kissing
dabble your bills
in holysobering water.

Where would I obtain in
winter flowers and where
the sunshine
and shadows of earth?
The walls stand
speechless and cold in wind
twisting the vanes.

"*Well* – bring him to me!"
Eleven years old
and we found the man

sitting at a long
narrow table near
the window – working.

For a time he looked
solemnly at us
and had a few words

with my dear teacher
and then was silent
when I went and played

a short piece by Ries.
Then he asked could I
play a fugue by Bach.

I chose the Fugue in
C Minor and then –
"Could you transpose it

into another
key at the same time?"
Happily I could.

After – I looked up.
His eyes fixed on me
broodingly and then

suddenly he smiled –
came over to me –
bent and stroked my head:

"Devil! And so young!"
Emboldened by this:
"May I play something

of yours now?" He smiled
nodding and I played
the C Major Con-

certo. Completed –
he took both my hands –
kissed me on the brow

and very gently –
"Off you go! Lucky
fellow – for you are

to provide joy and
happiness to so
many others. And

there's nothing better
or greater than that."
This occasion has

remained the crown of
my whole career. (Told
rarely – only – friends.)

FOUR COMMUNICATIONS
FROM HENRY DAVID

1
"Mimic idiom" –
study's furnishing
reminds all do well

to learn to speak the
living word – not some
trivial success –

little a little
better. Husks and shells
we make conquest of

for the most part or
most apparently –
but sometimes these are

cinnamon – spices –
you know. Even the
hunter you speak of

who slays a thousand
buffalo – brings off
only hides and tongues.

What sacrifices –
what hecatombs – what
holocausts the gods

exact for favors!
How much sincere life
can utter one word.

2
The American
can indeed cut down
and grub up all this

waving forest and
make a stump speech and
vote for Buchanan

on its ruins but
cannot converse with
the spirit of what

he deserts – nor read
the poetry he
retires progressing.

He ignorantly
erases tablets
of mythology

to print his handbills
and warrants. Before
he has learned his A

B C beautiful
mystic lore of the
wilderness Dante

and Spenser had just
begun to read he
coins a pine-tree cent

(pine's value to him) –
puts up a *dee*strict
schoolhouse and to prove

his having improved
things introduces
Webster's spelling book.

3
Will you break your heart
to save your neck? Necks
and pipestems are to

be broken. We men
make a great ado
about the folly

of asking too much
of life – or is it
of eternity?

and of trying to
live accordingly.
No harm ever came

of that. I dont fear
exaggerating
the value and sense

of life but of not
being up to its
occasion. Lived in

a golden age a
hired hand – visited
Olympus but fell

asleep at dinner's
end and didnt catch
the conversation

of the gods. Lived in
Judaea eighteen
hundred years ago

but never knew Christ
was one amongst my
contemporaries.

So if you have some-
thing to say to me –
please communicate.

4
Here's a theme for you:
To state to yourself
precisely fully

what climbing over
the mountains meant or
amounted to. Dont

suppose to do it
the first dozen times
you try – but at 'em

again and again –
especially when –
after enough pause –

you suspect you are
touching the summit
of the matter and

there account for the
mountain to yourself.
Not that the story

need be long – but it
takes time to make it
short. It didnt take

long to get over
the mountain – you thought?
But have you – indeed –

got over it? If
you've been to the top
of Mount Washington –

what did you find there?
Going up there and
being blown on is

nothing. It's after
we're home we really
go over it – if

we ever do. So –
what did the mountain
say – what did it do?

NO CONSOLATION

I dont know
why we live –
but believe

we can go
on living
because life's

finally
all we know
anything

about. In
other words
consciousness

is power –
though it may
seem at times

to be pure
misery.
Yet the way

it propa-
gates itself
from wave to

wave so that
we never
cease to feel –

though sometimes
we appear
to – try to –

pray to – there
is something
holding one

in one's place –
makes it a
standpoint in

the cosmos
probably
wise not to

forsake. We
are – yes – all
echoes of

the *same*. But
dont – please – too
much gener-

alize these
feelings – each
life is its

own special
problem – so
be content

with your own
terrible
algebra.

Dont melt in-
to the u-
niverse –

but be as
solid and
dense and fixed

as you can.
Sorrow comes
in great crests

and it rolls
over us
and almost

smothers us –
yet leaves us
on the spot

and we know
that if it
is strong we

are stronger:
it passes –
we remain.

It wears us –
uses us –
but we wear

it – use it
in return
and it is

blind whereas
we – after
a manner –

see. But wait.
We will help
each other.

You have my
tenderest
affection

and all my
confidence.
Henry James.

LEDA

After the god had realized his need
he was abashed to find himself a swan –
he felt himself confused at coming on
so – but now the disguise drew him to the deed

before understanding the wakening
creature's feeling. And she at the dawn
perceived now his coming into the swan
and knew now: he wanted something

she – bewildered in her opposing stance –
no longer could keep from him. He came down
and pushing past her ever weaker hands

lost his godhead in the belovedest.
Then he first found happiness in his down
and truly became swan within her nest.

THE MASTURAH

Here beyond the ridge
the path broke down
into a plain
opening

seaward. By the road
pilgrims had built
cairns – three stones on
each other –

common heaps to which
in passing we
who wished might add
another –

not reasonably –
nor knowing why
but assuming
others knew.

Whose house has burned down?
And whose is being –
feeling need deepen –

built anew? Is his
the heart rejoices
over every stone?

But if there never was
such a house and such
a fire and no rock?

If there is only
this body and this
hammered hammering

heart and those others
equally bereft
of any place to

call their own – what is
one to build? And still
one hears the word and

where is it coming
from and why does it
keep crying: *Rejoice!*

Not the sundown's
nicotine-stained
blood my ink nor

the abacus
the girl clicks but
the hot human

contorted mouth
indignantly
protesting "No" . . .

Schubert water, Mozart birds,
Goethe whistling twistingly,
Hamlet meditating steep,
sensed our pulse and trusted it.

Perhaps my whisper was con-
ceived before my lips and leaves
treelessness and you my life
long before you came to this.

To Drury –
his doctor
pupil friend:

"I would like
to say – or
write – this: Don't

think about
yourself but
your patients.

You said that
possibly
you had made

a mistake
in having
taken up

medicine:
and added –
probably

it was wrong
to think so.
I'm sure. But

not because
being a
doctor you

may not go
wrong or to
the dogs but

because no
one can say
what would have

been right if
this is wrong.
You did your

best. Now: live
in the world
in which you

are – not the
world in which
you would like

to be. Look
at people's
sufferings –

they are the
remedy
for your pains.

Rest when you
ought to and
let yourself

34

come to rest.
(Not with me:
I wouldnt

rest you.) Look
at patients
more closely

as human
beings in
trouble and

enjoy more
the chance you
have to say

'Good night' to
so many.
This alone

many would
envy you
and this will

heal your soul –
I believe.
In talk with

me dont so
much try to
think of what

goes down well
(that you will
never get)

but what leaves
the freshest
aftertaste.

Central is
not to have
wasted a

single day
we could have
together.

I wish you
good thoughts – more:
good feelings."

II

MERCY

Come into
the darkness to
find this figure

standing only
slightly bowed with
eyes carved blind

seeing beyond
and through our eyes
the light so

one hand weigh
and the other
extend shadow.

Uncanny
precision
to have set

stone upon
stone so and
concave and

convex this
adjoined twelve-
cornered one

still holding
the world up
from conquest.

THE SCENARIO

We always seem
to come in in
the middle and

never stay to
see the end – though
we do assume

or at least feel
there is an end –
as there was a

beginning – but
of course we arent
sure of either

or even that
this is amidst
anything we

have a right to
think of as an
event. Which brings

us to wonder
why we ever
came anyhow

and what – being
here – we're supposed
to do? Even

more we wonder
who the question
is for – and what

an answer might
mean. Beyond what
in fact it does.

MACBETH

Tomorrow and tomorrow *and* tomorr-
ow – what he meant – what he felt – what we know
unable to move beyond the event

of our own eventuality. Duns-
inane. Guttering body – guttering
shadow – nothing at last at last nothing.

THE ARTIST

All he had hoped for
was to paint the white
until the white ap-

peared in all its white
until the very
black of it came out

and all color felt
precisely what it
had – to become – light.

Just a chunk of wood –
ax like a chisel
put to it – hacking

away the form and
face of a smile whose
wisdom confronts us

with stroke upon stroke
of what it meant to
be making Enku.

STUDENT

Sitting at the sea
absorbed in it – a
Tolstoy with Gorki

coming up behind –
hearing the silence
break upon the shore.

RELIC

Conferoax
implexa –
in a fine hand

penciled on
the yellowing
endpaper

of a Book – a
Bournemouth gift
long afterward

aired over –
via Vermont
to Kyoto –

sample of a
seaweed an
old salt kept as

a token
perhaps – a
particular

tress – of one of
the myriad
Nereids

48

whose escapades
daunted hearts
as fond as his

or – likelier –
what it is –
a specimen.

Someone has to win
the lottery. O Lord –
let it not be me!

This is the trouble
with the poet who
prays for poverty –

who wouldnt buy a
ticket to the hall
of fame and only

sneaks into the old
Abbey to see where
a friend is buried.

I think of him
always dying –
saying as much

disregarded.
Complaining of
neglect and hard

on those who cared
enough not to
forget. But what

does the sun want
of us – apart
from what it takes?

FOUR COMMUNICATIONS
FOR GEORGE

1
What I like about him is
the honesty of his words –

letting them be poetry –
not making anything of

what the words make but aware
of what they are – occurring

the way sun water breath skin
feel upon emerging from

a good swim in the ocean –
the sense of having come clean.

Even the sand underfoot
seems consonant with one's weight.

2

He will always be
the poet – silent –
against the edge of

that leap upward of
rock facing at sun-
down the Pacific –

not looking brave or
solicitous but
glad – grateful. Human.

3 PILGRIMS

I think I know what
George means when he says
"There are words that mean

nothing – but there is
something to mean." He
still bears the faith and

the marks of that faith
in him. Not unlike
delight in the green

he sees strike up from
the sidewalk in spite
of it. And I in

turn delight in his
recognition – though
I have had to leave

that country – abused
beyond my power
to struggle against

for being stupid
enough to trust in
those I live with. You.

4

Like trying to speak
to George and fully
aware his death stops

here. He wanted so
much – as we want – some-
thing good to happen

to people – for them
to be kind – to be
what he continued

to feel they could be –
clear as anything –
as the night which has –

even as I write
these words looked up from –
suddenly appeared.

TABLEAU VIVANT

That anything is:
you know what I mean –
the dusty winesap

sitting too long in
Doug's bowl among the
sour oranges –

rotten to the core –
but gifted with a
scent of having been

part of the living
tree – the deep dark red
skin flecked with white and

suggesting the flesh
within. Still there on
the table. Still life.

Suddenly
a bird call
makes it seem

(I dont know
why) like a
holiday –

like getting
a letter
from Lorine.

Paul Celan also
meant to be human
but death was too much

to make meaning of –
not at least without
entering into.

I can no
more eat for
than die for

you but Bill's
plums still taste
good to me.

EXCURSION

From Moline
to nearly
Keokuk

on Mark Twain's
river on
John Deere's yacht –

millionaires
for a day –
reveling

in the sun-
set – certain
it was made

for those who
see to it
and return

to it. Like
death. Strangers
reminded

of how far
this is is
to have been.

REMEMBERING BARI

How the prickles doused
glisten – a sphere all
crown. It hurts to be

and not to have been
hurts – knowing – more. Fruit
of the sea – urchin.

THE SKEIN

How much I would give
(give) to be sitting –
arms extended – palms

parallel – fingers
tight – thumbs up – holding
a hank of washed yarn

Mother now winds off
into a quick ball –
into the whole piece.

III

The ant waits
and I wait
upon its
majesty.

AVANT-GARDE

Leaving us
all these years
to see through

seeing you
all these years
that evening

on the fence
on last leave
calling to

us and us
calling good
bye and by

the darkness
lit by a
cigarette.

Like a child again
holding a round stone
in my hand until

the warmth of my hand
warms the stone and I
feel comprehended.

I've grown up.
I'm into
you. Like the

first time the
taste of the
"the" the teeth

a little
deterred – breath
coming through.

ENURESIS

Terror is not – Ed –
sitting in one's piss.
I know – I've sat there –

I've slept there and did
most of my childhood.
That was warmth – in fact –

and comfort – in spite
of the unconcealed
unconcealable

smell. Terror? That was
and always will be
Mother cursing Dad

and there there I am
alone in that night
hearing that door slam.

I'm shitting
alone – at home.
Naturally

the telephone
rings and rings and
rings – wont wipe

it: first things first.
Which takes as
long as it takes.

THE DETAIL

If I dont do it
someone else
must. The men

pumping the muck out
need it flushed
to flow. Not

the sweetest
labor but
flavor of its own.

Someone I cared for
put it to me: Who
do you think you are?

I went down the list
of all the many
possibilities

carefully – did it
twice – but couldnt find
a plausible one.

That was when I knew
for the first time who
in fact I wasnt.

The kettle steaming
on the hob – the hob
in this case being

a small gas stove to
heat the room. Bubbles
rattling the silence

reminding me that
every word used will
be used against me.

The hills move with me.
A little farther
ahead or beside

or behind – as I
take the turns to and
from Takao. They

say nothing to me
patiently. That's what
I like about them.

KINDRED

Once when I was
I thought of you
not yet born and

wasnt certain
if what I had
to say could have

any meaning
for you. I know
even less now

or nothing – but
if you must be
here you need this

confirmation
as much as I
do – writing it.

THE WILL

Hard to tell you or
anyone I dont
want anything. It's

all I can do to
try to dispose of
what possesses me.

Cid said something
like this. He's dead –
you know – died long

ago. Strange how
near the words come
sometimes to what

seemed so remote.
As if you felt
yourself at home.

Just a cold wind
whipping my face
trying to catch

my breath in the
uphill struggle
from being out

in it to the
chance of a rest
when I get home.

ELEUSIS

I look at you and
I dont understand –
I dont profess to –

the same person who
nearly out of her
skull a year ago

came back to this – her
home – and now is whole
again – can again

pretend to be here
and I still with you
astonishingly.

No wonder the leaves
November colors
cheer me quietly.

THE PACKAGE

I had to
die. Not a
need but a

possession –
what was in
the body

like a prize –
sur-prise. Not
the candy.

Being here
proves nothing.
Nothing I

say or can
can put off
the nothing

each breath takes
and gives back
nothing to.

SHO

This instrument
gets to me as
no other does –

the music of
breathing lifting
beyond silence

the strain of what
it means to be
an instrument.

You touch me
and I grow –
you take me

and I am –
we are no
one alone.

No one to take me
by the hand – no one
to be there with me

and yet all await
all. All . . . To speak of
snow as the snow falls.

Not the image of
the swimmer – my dad –
swimming out over

his head – plunging there –
feet pointing up a
moment and then – strange –

instead of the straight
swim back to shore or –
stranger – the long swim

out and out and out
and out – making the
horizon – strangest

of all – he swims – he
swims towards me and
swims without gaining

on the shore – and swims
while I stand there and
you become – and swims.

IV

THE TRANSMISSION

Sitting
in
an ashram

Katmandu
moon
summit

thinking
of writing
you.

90

COGITO ERGO
COGITO SUM

A hand
out for
a snowflake

or how
a hand
understands.

The crushed butts
at the bus
stop next to

the trash can.
So much more
than we can

compass or
ever get
away from.

Do we need all this
solitude just to
feel comfortable

in being able
to fart? We are much
too magnificent.

THE

mosquito
at the ear
saying so
so and so.

To have a flower
in the house. The dead
blossoming. The last

time. As if the sun
came through the window
pirouetted here.

Walking through a wood
coming out upon
a stream – the running

light – the shrine path to
the vast green cage (whack
whack) of a golf range.

POIGNANCE

Over the gas jet
my wife cremating
a pregnant cockroach.

All at once it glows
and glows again – the
point of any point.

KAERU

There's our little
Buddha squatting
on a leaf

all body a
breath swelling to
protect it.

The world is not theirs:
they are animals.
You're sentimental.

I'm sentimental.
The world is not ours:
we are animals.

Old pine –
roots crushed
by concrete –

cut down –
removed. Who
recalls

the absence
of a
shadow?

Shadow of cloud
on shadow of
hill. Veil on veil

dancing – lifting
ahead – bringing
the gift of sight

its distances
and nakedness –
the failure to

create the thing
it is – to let
the morning be.

Light touches
each of us
for shadow

We dont lend
but all that
we are gives.

Feeling what it means
to have arisen:
we are the thorns whose
roses are his blood.

Hey – it
aint just
any

one who
dies: it's
you. That's

what makes
today
so clear.

Now
the glazed look on
the bird's face

The sense of
something beyond –
flesh.

That feeling
of snow and
whether it

comes – or not
feeling it
there – as if

it were the
air but as
that much more.

If these words be ours
and the words nothing –
as they are – then we

are nothing too. Yes –
yes – let it be so.
But let the words know.

The bell rings
from the hill
human time

There is no
other – no
other sound.

SENSEI

Only an old man
sitting on the ground
striking the lute and

singing the story
of another time
making one of it.

It isnt just
the silence. The
sky itself seems

at this moment
incredibly
true. As if it

had without a
single word said
all that it could.

V

Sky at the window.
Breath obeying breath.
At home in a house.

Out of nowhere –
or so it seems
to these eyes –

on bare boughs
a galaxy
of chickadees.

GYOKURO

An old lady in
kimono bringing
a tray with the tea

very delicious
and carefully brewed
for only a sip

of the flavor of
the dim room of her
family temple.

When was this to be?
The first leaves of the
cutback hydrangea

are opening. The
earth is like a fist
threatening nothing.

Wisteria
the accouterment
of a bride

without the bride.
But the wedding
still goes on.

THE PRESENTATION
OF THE VIRGIN

On the table
in a vase
a rose

It all
seems to have
been decided.

All those bees
busy at
azaleas

goddam sure
of what they
are about.

Sky in
the puddle –

dog lapping
it up.

The I Ching the rain.
Let the drops fall
where they will and

let them lie there –
a fortune just
as the sun foretold.

Rain fell
a moment
ago

stopped for
a moment
now.

Two
half-submerged
rowboats

oarless
weeds the sky
floats.

Whose fault
or any?
Why pick

on apples
when dust
bruises air?

A
cricket

making
it

The
cricket.

What is life – or death?
Nothing – to explain.

JOB

Patience is
rewarded:
nothing comes.

ALPHONSE/GASTON

One leaf after another.
Or is it each before each?

Nothing
to do –
seeing

the leaf
come down –
but see.

Every
leaf and twig
twist of the

tree reveals
what goes on
within goes

on within
a larger
circuit yet.

Takes
little but
the little

all –
every
night night falls.

Finally
snow – setting
the scene for

silence and
maybe a
footstep out.

Moon the flute –
man the drums –
the sun is
coming out.

Already
dawn: when call
it a day

This is as
good a time
as any.

Utano
12 December 1984